AND CARET BAY AGAIN

NEW AND SELECTED POEMS

ALSO BY VELMA POLLARD

Poetry

Crown Point
Shame Trees Don't Grow Here
The Best Philosophers I Know Can't Read or Write
Leaving Traces

Fiction

Karl and Other Stories
Homestretch

Other Prose

Considering Woman
Considering Woman 1 and 2

Non-fiction

Dread Talk: The Language of Rastafari
From Creole to Standard

ACKNOWLEDGEMENTS

The poems from *The Best Philosophers I know Can't Read and Write* (2001) appear by kind permission of Mango Publishing.

VELMA POLLARD

AND CARET BAY AGAIN

NEW AND SELECTED POEMS

P E E P A L   T R E E

First published in Great Britain in 2013
Peepal Tree Press Ltd
17 King's Avenue
Leeds LS6 1QS
UK

© Velma Pollard 2013

ISBN 13: 9781845232092

Supported by
ARTS COUNCIL
ENGLAND

CONTENTS

From *The Best Philosophers I know Can't Read or Write*

From *Leaving Traces*

New Poems

To my grandchildren:

Stephanie, Stephen, Brianna, Amari and Manuel

from

CROWN POINT

1988

CROWN POINT

The sea hums endlessly
Stars through the darkness
wake my homespun peace…

'…A see mi great granfather
jumping hopscotch and playing marble…'

I see MY grandmother praying

'…Bless the Lord oh my soul
and all that is within me
bless his holy name…'

and the round green world of penny-royal
smells the room
through windows cool and sweet
and khus-khus from the cupboard
counter smells.

On the shelf her pan
a miniature suitcase black and red
with stamps and old receipts and dust
there too her bible large and black
its file of leaves in red
turned to us kneeling
this bible full…
God's words and other words
birth dates and marriages
and deaths

'… and forget not all his benefits
who forgiveth all thy iniquities
who healeth all thy diseases
who satisfieth thy mouth with good things…'

Thus speaks my Gran
through this Tobago silence…
and recreates the order of her room
and recreates the aura of her God
and speaks so clearly in me…

Perhaps the clutter of my life
obscures her voice
Perhaps the clutter of my mind
frustrates her
streaming to my consciousness
Perhaps her mystic to me
waits my silence
waits my tomorrows' spaces.

NATIONAL HEROES 1980

How many Baptist heads must young Salome seek
because she danced the Horah for a king?

how many times must tumbrils
rumbling pass from lady guillotine?

how many Jewless houses Hitler do you ask?

how many Blacks must dot the middle stream?

how many corpses dangling in the wind
must feed their stench
must poison all this land
before you retributive givers
cancelling plagues
call off your hounds of hell?

SUNDAY THOUGHTS (FRENCHMAN'S COVE)

Troubled with ologies
the paper tigers claw us and each other
raking the muck that smells in tier on tier
poisoning the land

but in the cove where almond trees
orelias and their parasites hang cool
where blue/green
gently hugs the jutting rock-face
every second splash
or lover-rough and hungry
hurls whiteness on its grey
calm holds the earth

beyond
space hides the ripples
blue/green marble
stretches to a boundless edge
unless a smart canoeist
sudden turns his boat
and somehow marks
that something ends here
or begins

that smooth sea
hides the litter of a thousand earths
washed in by earthquake storm or tidal wave
perhaps
the sea will wash our land
perhaps
destruction with its blessed cleansing
will call our country
to a baptism.

FISHERMAN

Fisherman
you know your net
you know the ill-starred puffed-up fish
who swims with confidence
flexing his fins

Smile walrus fisherman
and weep with motions
casting out your net
spreading its glassy weave
and waiting, waiting patiently
till flexed fins rest
till confidence relaxes on the weave

then watch your hapless catch
squirm on the wooden surface
of your quaint canoe
its fish-eyes crazed in wonder
So many many ill-starred mates

BUD/UNBUDDED

This bud beheld me watch
her glory folded
This bud beheld me move one minute spot in time
Unbudded/outrose/her petals myriading…

This flower sees me watch
her glory flaunted
This flower hears me pause
and knows I pause to grieve for her tomorrows' spaces.

BIRD KISS

blue grey
my bright noon sky
twin birds
identical from here
and black rush to each other
clutch
then quickly disengage

quick kiss
beneath the feathers
in the high noon sun?
quick snarl beneath the feathers
in the harsh noon sun?

I favour love
black boy black girl
bird kiss me quick
then laughing wing vault
through the blue grey sky

MOODS

I

Night

The trombone's last note
dies; the drum's timpano trembles;
the drummer's hand
still lightly rests upon his wand.

Put up your instruments
the concert's over
the lights are going out
the sounds fade into memory
to rise again
but later much much later…
the darkness fogs me round
I cannot find a road
to home.

II

Morning

Hanging in
learning my hurt
while you grow
glow worms
through our mutual night

Hanging in
dawn now
my new birth
breaching; its cords
hanging hope

Morning
my tenuous yellow
let eyes light
and shine me
to growth again.

FLY

ef a ketch im
a mash im
ef a ketch im
a mash im
ef a ketch im...

Will you walk into my parlour
Said the spider to the fly
It's the prettiest snugliest parlour
That ever you did spy... And I
the fly
inspecting your web
this skein now then that
put my microscope eye
through its intricate weave
saw valleys of cloud
blue and serene
saw acres of grass
sheltered and green.
Ephemeral and light
I rested my life
and dazzled
I watched
you wove me inside
and dazzled
I slept
my crysalis sleep...

* * *

I woke up inside
no more dazzled and green.
Awake and alert
unfolding my wings
I stretched

But your skeins
not delicate now
resistant and strong
they wove me inside
I am trapped
I can't move
I can't butterfly
fly

And you
perched outside
your eyes large and clear
you see acres of green
you see valleys of cloud
you can move
you can fly...
Now I look through the web
I look into the void
I see numberless flies
training microscope eyes
through intricate weave
ANANSI I cry
ANANSI-SI-SI I hear
the sky is too vast
how it scatters my cry
the sky is too clear
it hides my despair
they can't hear
they can't see
with their microscope eye...

ef a ketch im
a mash im
ef a ketch im
a mash im

A ketch im... im... im

21

AFTER CAGES

Behind remembered Sunday papers
sits my father's grunts
rain patter or the sharp uneven crunch
of children's feet toeing the gravel
Mulvina's off again (I hear her say)...
Did you remember, called your mother yesterday?...
and chews more firmly on his latest pipe.

After the patter
after children's tired toes
the silent Sunday
thunders this bird's exit
leaving her window-peering silent
newly old.

Someday I'd say
she'll up and go
leaving him window-peering under rain
drops chewing pipes
at home
no going when it's no one that you are leaving.

Behind these Sunday papers
sits my father's silence now
hearkening the raindrops' patter
or the pebbles empty of remembered feet;
parsley and mint fragrant where I remember
brown pipes and brown tobacco littering the ash

Soundless we sit
silent and impotent
who is Mulvina?
where his mother now?
I know no questions

feel no urge to learn
too late I know
he needs to answer
lonely women newly old
but oddly silenced now
stretched out beside the flowers
boxed brown in aged mahogany.

ANANSA

IM no PERCEPT
how ABLE-Y
Anansa weaves
the only web she knows
around my house
(and not because
the house is mine)
she weaves because she must
the urge to weave comes in...
my house as if on wheels
goes out...

Anansa's threads are thin
and strong
so thin I can't perceive (nor he)
until I feel my house begin to move
pulled off, destabilised
by threads of magic web

He's on his hupentery
deep inside his desk
his space is changeless
till (and after many thoughts)
he steps outside...

the wind already cold
the neighbours gone beyond return
a new environ-
ment to blow his mind...

Empire fragments
in marble as in men.
The marble reconnects
but humpty dumpty's

fragments cannot hold.
The king tiif, the governor tiif
me tiif, you tiif, all a we tiif.
The king is forever a woman.

DEJA VUE (FOR DEEP)

there near that shattered stone
now hardly fit for two
silence and moonscape
touched our tenderness

later
that dream grew
silence slept
and voices rising
steps their vague
pat-patter
children
like fresh plants sprung
like flowers glowing
wildly from our earth

an end-
less time
and yet you kept me comfort
with your
soon
these times will be
like dots on our remembering
calmness come over all

now near that stone again
moonscape and silence
voices and footfall
mimic our memory
silence
now dreamless
that dream grew rich
to fill our silence
with its bounty.

HINDSIGHT II

if there were space enough
to hold our different lives
within one love
if there were myriad golden rings
molded into our ceremony…

so leaving you
I took the ring
savoured its smoothness
fingering its face
until my frightened nail
released its secret catch
snapped wide its circle
there
a clover
FIVE leafed
perfect sprang
mirabile. I crossed myself
and whispering trembling thanks
I snapped it close.

SCREWS LOOSE

I do not wish to sit and smile
too sweetly where the pavement ends
nor set small windy fires at Papine
nor scrupulously cleanse myself in streams
guttering too slowly
gathering stench on stench

I do not wish to mumble as I go
gesturing wildly as the voice grows old
eyes staring wide
and crude uneasy laugh

mad people whisper late
sane people's early dreams
beware my inmost thoughts
that wait mad mind's release

too much too soon
the mind rejects it all
uncensored now and overflowing here
flotsam and jetsam mixed with precious pearl

and so my love my seraph dear go home
mad women whisper sane men's names
and not in jest
leave me my dreams of growing calmly old
turning thin pages in moth-ridden books
rocking my evening bones
watching each sun go down

BRITISH MUSEUM AND AFTER

Guardian of the Great Tradition
those volumes stood
in sturdy black
and through their golden teeth of leaves
sent whispers down:
pass gently gently
touch me not
touch me not for I am holy

Guardian of a great tradition
those statues stood
remembering Egypt
and from the stone lips of the sphinx
the silent whisper
touch me not
and pass me gently
I am cold and I am lonely
I am freezing naked poorly
for I need the golden desert
need its parching on my stone

From the hollow of that sound
from the screaming of that rape
to the shelter of my nothing…

Then the voice of that other
took my hand in his invisible hand
and led me to the bed of the river
where little banks like dunes of sand
sit waterless in the river's lap
and over my head his inaudible voice:
this is the voice of the waterless river
this is the voice of the shallow peaks
these are the books of endless unbinding…

And the voice of his hand
held my hand firm and led me
to my timeless children
who played in their present
Tannique and Tungi
Kamau and Abenna

Show them your river
said his soundless voice
show them the dunes
the dry sanded bank-heads
the clear mountain trickle
that tomorrow will fall
white foam falls of beauty
let them play in this present
where the grass greens low
and the silt land is ready

And these books of endless unbinding
will fatten with the leaves of their reaping
and the seamless wide open wall sides
will green with the pages of their toil…
tomorrow belongs to the children.

REMEMBERING WASHINGTON DC

In Washington
Black DC
not to be confused with
Washington White DC
one Sunday
I saw God

Yes I saw God
in clothes He wouldn't recognise
in every habit man has ever worn
I saw Him ageing bald
with three-piece suit bow-tie
I saw Him robed in purple black and brown
and then I saw Him beating Babylon down
strutting and young
and under flowing gown
complete with fez to crown
His black hamitic face

and He got poorer
as His clothes got looser
until He sat on stoops
and rapped with sisters
smelling of incense
blackness and conversion
where Florida merged with
Georgia on my mind (?)

Sunday
down Florida
I knew
Black folks have God
White folks have

at least
in Washington
DC

BELIZE SUITE

I: Sea Wall

Only a gentle swish
Where waves would touch the land
no wind no turbulence
along this wall arranged by man
dividing land from sea

No cruise-ships light this harbour end
to end only that cluster
where the army lights
ride there at anchor…
cool darkness and deluding calm

houses sit silent near the water's edge
their calm precarious like our peace
hoisted on stilts
like mokojumbies in the carnival
listening the ocean's gentle murmur
hearing its angry wail
what seems like decades now
when death rode loud and furious
on the hissing waves

From storm and earthquake Lord
deliver us
and us
and us

II: Xunantunich (for Roy W)

The gods will ask
tell them I left my offering there
three handspans to the left
of that dread corner where the two slabs meet
under a stone
set in a threadbag
that I kept between my breasts
so that my hands could help me
timid goat
climb halfway up
no more

it isn't strength that matters
courage to climb
is what the old hearts lose
my children's children never now will know
what sights the high-priests saw
undizzied by the dizzying heights

Power is always from on high
lookouts where pirates guard the harbour
rivers that tumble down from angry hills
cloud tops for cherubim
and Maya priests' Xunantunich

III: Road from Xunantunich

Dusk settles in
first near the edge
where towns like pale mirages sit
and only slowly shrouds us
shocked to silence by the stillness here…

Where are the night sounds
that begin at dusk?
not here or just not yet?

King trees with long and hairless trunks
reach green and fertile locks
towards the sky

no mountains here no rocks
no green between those thick locks
and the close cropped kinks
that can't protect the land
cracked now with long unsightly breaks
(the geolog unstraps his EYE and clicks)

Who would be king
but with no subjects
who would grow strong and perfect
but alone?

This silence sobers us
and sends us feverish
seeking home

IMPRESSIONS – HAVANA 1979

And what is there to see
so long after the last of the marines
the last of modish cars
the last of fashionable dames
liquid with moonlit glasses
or sequined underneath harsh lights
and urgent hands?

It is an empty city
clean streets where many lanes
lie mocking swift pedestrian feet
that follow glances upstreet and downstreet
expectantly

but no cars come
large overcrowded buses
hurry workers tired
to their dormitories
as evening settles in

and bright lights now
no longer usher in the night.

II

It was Manhattan
                without the cars
It was Madrid
                without the bull-ring
and so perhaps
I felt a body vacant
waiting for its animus

this city that Espana must have loved
to mark her image here tan cuidosamente
where Yankis must have drunk delight
so deep
that they would wish
to recreate their citadel
their Casa Blanca
near this perfect sea

But I want to celebrate
the animus this city waits
now springing
sweet and slender
clear-eyed
children

for I have listened to them work in learning centres
and I have watched them playing in the squares
and they have made me listen in the streets
almost as if they knew
that I would want to sense
their budding...

Tomorrow I will visit Havana again
when the spirit full-blown
inhabits the city

and I will hear the city talk
and I will forget Manhattan
I will forget Madrid
I will hear Havana... de Cuba.

III

The great mulatto nation disappears
after the belch of the tunnel
al avenida del puerto

Aquí in old Havana
little blacks
our old men toothless
smiling solidarity… verdad
our children
none too clean
flooding the plazas
near the cathedral
God once called his own
the children none too clean
but fed… verdad
and thank God
smiling confidence

We have become accustomed to finding us
in the kitchens of large cities
we have become accustomed to finding us
on the docks of large cities

and so these old men
smiling toothless
nodding memories
of seas they sailed
old salts
watching their grandsons
tumble near the flagstones
don't surprise us here
allà in my Jamaica
street-light children
scrounge 'beg you a ten cents nuh'

black angels
hungry angels

these angels here
they smile
they eat
they play
their good abuelos
toothless sit
but smile.

LONG MOUNTAIN

(Travelogue for Rooftops and George R)

I

too young
too new
too far
too future
books clutter my spaces
Long Mountain shoulder
shelter me
plodding
this innocent beat
to your warm open hill-door

II

white
bright
coldlight fresh snow-
flakes printless
waiting footfall
waiting ploughfall
this land breeds tyrants
Long Mountain shoulder
show me your green mind
melting this lovelessness

III

Manhattan brick on claustro-
phobic
brick
thrown up
near sky
line
underground rumblings
black tikki tikki
white tikki tikki
dock in their destiny
Long Mountain shoulder
hug close my psyche

IV

roads rush to river
roads rush to sea-
wall canals to koker
swamps swell this land
spaced mudtide to landedge
cottages crawl
horizon hunting
watch where their fathers
hunted your fathers
hiding
hoping
endless this openness
fitted you fatalist…
maronage mock me
Long Mountain shoulder
hide me in history
maronage make me

V

maronage waiting
Long Mountain hold me
leaning this shudder
quaked on your shoulder
pine green above me
pine smell all over me
mist and the morning
mend this cracked spirit
fit firm this wild mind
splintered with wandering
Long Mountain hug me
hushed on your shoulder
maronage shelter me
maronage make me

SUSU

Susu su su   Susu su su
among the yellow poui
you hear
I hear
leaves in the Japanese garden
'tiday fi mi tumaro fi yu'
like Brer Anancy talking in his nose
Susu su su

And how 1 laughed that day
I heard them say
'im shouldn bury there
im a go come back fi dem have no fear'
denying all the rural wisdom I had known…

Then quick and fast
some hidden hit man
strikes us off our anxious lists
and you
and I
stand open-mouthed
as poui leaves whisper just before they fall

  tiday fi mi
  tumaro fi yu
  Susu su su
  Susu su su

OUR MOTHER
(for Lixie)

'*Strew on her roses roses*
And never a touch of yew…'

Orange and red for our mother
who sang us bright songs…
jigging from side to side
pointing her index fingers
doing the Bustamante
the K-walk ('Cake' they correct me now)
and tuned (perhaps an octave high)
that 'you can't hinder me
from loving you…'

who stored long poems
neatly script
in her best blackboard hand
and fancy scrap books
weddings full
used press books
pasted over
pop songs
fit for a younger queen(?)
'Butterflies green butterflies blue
Oh how they flutter up and butter up for you…'
and mixed the ages endlessly
flowing each generation into each
'South of the border
dont mestik away…'
(I couldnt figure that
till I could read
and scrap-book settled it
'down Mexico way')

45

then I saw broad black hats
and squat young yellow men
winking their eyes
in lies
saying mañana…

No tears
no sad songs
for our lady
who jigged from this life
into that
and did not wave adieu…

Endless and timeless
rediscoveries
headfuls of history
voicefuls of song
duets and trios
moonshine and mystery…
watch di moonshine baby man
still sitting there in the morning

and hid her hardships
underneath the fictive griefs
of Lucy Gray, Lord Ullin's child,
Mary Maguire
who stole three loaves
and drove the judge to tears…
all suffering whites
she didnt know nor cared
or else conveniently forgot
insisting still
unquestioned Coromanti
and did not live to have them tell her
she was not.

TO GRAN... AND NO FAREWELL

I didnt wish to see the moth-marks
where your Khus Khus smelled
the high weeds crowding the forget-me-nots
or alien fingers
handling knives and spoons
kept sheening in brown calico

and so I let the years
make jumbie chain-links
ages long
before I brought
bright florets for your grave

One room remains
and one small fretwork shard
among the rotted beams
ingrown with baby grass
remembers still the august Entry Hall
tributes of broken china
lean-to tables
and an old man
shambling out and in
cursing the vultures
who would snatch the land...

I round the corner
eager with my shrubs
the grave at last...
then unbelieving shudder
Corpie's tomb
Naomi's garden square
and yours that now
my mind will never hold

no single adoration
no peculiar tears
some well-intentioned
madman with his spade…
all now one vast sepulchraic mass

I crush the shrublets
tramp them underfoot
and with a heart
too swollen now for tears
descend the slope
without adieu.

from

SHAME TREES DON'T GROW HERE

1992

HEATHROW IN RETROSPECT

It wasnt the first time I was in Heathrow. It might have been the fourth or fifth. And I dont remember why I was there – meeting somebody, leaving or arriving myself I dont know but I was at the British Airways counter and gazed out along the concourse to behold, and quite unexpectedly, The British Empire on which the sun never sets.

Well what a revelation! Suddenly I felt that I was England called upon after all to put my money where my mouth lie (accepting the pun). All those on whom the sun had not set were along that concourse – ladies with head covers like hats beekeepers wear and mesh right down to the chin – people you were sure could never eat for all the tackle on nose and mouth nor go to the bathroom for all the skirt and trousers at their legs. There were dazzling saris there with brown love-handles smiling at ageing waists; black hair thrown open at the seam to accommodate one deep red spot and tall men each with his finely wrought fez walking as if flowing skirts and sandalled feet were help not hindrance to unreasonable speed.

No one had warned the British in their mad rush into Expansion that this contraction here at Heathrow would be likely. They had not then conceived of fast ships or of aeroplanes, linguistic skill and wild ambition that would bring all shades of black and brown (and white) to this one shelter and the cruel irony of children of the empire brothers all, at Heathrow.

And amid the bustle on Oxford Street, returning from the colonies now to retire, an old limey asks: 'Is there still space for an Englishman?'

DRAKE'S STRAIT REMEMBERED

After the Virgins
all seas all oceans
seem unreasonably bare
The Atlantic
Los Angeles to Santa Barbara
with only Catalina sitting there
At home
after Port Royal's blade
a few brief cays
and then the empty sea

Volcanic beauty
jagged edges
merging into
hilltops that were
beaches where the Taino played
wild blues of deep sea
gentle grey-green hills
marking horizons
that can shift and change
as yonder becomes here
under the helmsman's hand
rocks you can almost touch
that stand and speak to rock
and islets bobbing
out of nowhere
to become
a green girl in the ring
tra la la la laa

Earth and the sea
they know their business
change is not distress
here only beauty now
and calm

ROAD TO HARRIMAN UPSTATE NY

So often trees and copper rock-
face miles along
George Washington

trees leafless
like lace

And you have taught me rocks
fencing the sea
or settling underfoot of beach…

so now I see them large
waiting for carver to reborn them
Maya pyramids or small
tossed here and there as if a boulder
builder chipped and said
not you and you and you…
nestling behind the tree line
or jutting out before it
as we leave New York
in passionate adieu

II

brrbudum   brrbudum
the car repeats road ridges
built to live both sun and snow
hushing cold thoughts
with rhythms like the gentle hums
commuter throats control
(their good-conductor-bad-paymaster
good-conductor-bad-paymaster
Richmond to Port Antonio does anyone remember?)

III

Lake leaking
into limestone
making the rock
polished slate

nature on one hand
on the other man
his vulgar discount square

there's too much
everything
the landscape now begins
to cloy my island mind

until ascent
and the first deer
(so exquisitely carved)
bounds down in his perpetual wonder
stops
stands hands akimbo
taking in strange cars
then rushes back
to warn his brother
quell that panic
there akimbo too
three four five deer

Harriman and the double lions
white and couchant
welcome
in nineteenth century splendour

IV

But whose ancestors are these
lining the walls
with patient eyes?
heads
of head-hunters
hunted by Harrimans
(who rest in graves
fenced off below the boathouse?)

victims now
victors on the walls
these halls
where Tales from the
Vienna Woods
muffle the moan
of Mohawk and Seneca

where were the umpires
who were they
that such a carnage
built this empire?

Raindrops mingle with the fog

through wiremeshed glass
I notice spirits lighting on the limb

HARRIMAN REVISITED I

My ancestors
sit
head hung
eyes pinching into
eye lids
lips too thin to curl
arch down or
press firm lip on lip
in scorn where once
defiance sat
in vain

We
sit
head
hung
tired
from
fighting
for the
land
that is
not theirs
but the
Creator spirit's

Ancestors
like deer heads
trophies on the walls
these halls
opposing
tapestries
portray
their men
with maps
with axes
with theodolites
trees fallen
like Indian heads
Blood
Sarsi
Assinboin
Santo Domingo
Blackfoot
Blood
at Harriman

Heads
bowed
then broke
and fell
up to these
walls
grand-
daughter
where
you
see
us
CRY

HARRIMAN REVISITED II

Grandmother
I too cry
a hundred years
tears
for missing you
your wisdom
and your patient
beads

Holding my anger
in so I can now
take back with even hand
the goods they took
unoffered
from your hand
I sit
beneath these logs
of fire
your erstwhile woods
watching your eyes
begging your blessing
asking that you forgive
that I should come
should lightly trip
up these broad stairs
past trees
whose roots
were stained with blood
of Bloods
past doorways
stained again with blood
past lying smiles
frozen on lips
of grandsons of this house

saying they wish me well
who never wished
nor me
nor you
not anything
but hell

MY DAUGHTER RESEMBLES
HARRY BELAFONTE'S DAUGHTER

Upstate New York
morning and March
fog filtering through
leafless trees
delicate like lace
and I see Montreal
fog
and all that snow on the ground
young fresh snow
soon to age
downtrodden under wheel and foot
and leafless branches
hung heavy with ice

But it is Upstate New York
and no more Montreal
than my daughter is Harry Belafonte's daughter
only the stereotype caucasians see
of a young woman
confident with low cut negro hair
like the stereotype I see
of fog and French lace
formed in winter trees

BAG WOMAN

Bag Winter
rain woman
perhaps I know
how ungentle
is snow
how wet
hurting your furniture
that's neither wood nor wicker
cloth and card-
board will whimper
not stand up
in Winter rain
Woman

LION

I believe
that the lion on the sphinx
is couchant

I have not seen
the sphinx

Four weeks in Britain's kingdom
I have seen
at least four hundred lions
rampant
arrogant
flagrant
ram
panting like dragon
puffing flames
from flaring nostrils

the sphinx
without his nose
(they tell me s/he is
defaced)
can neither puff
nor pant

and coming from a culture
valuing much
respect
and valuing much less
rampant arrogance
(even the lion of Judah
Ethiopia's pride
is standing on four feet
and does not romp

nor vaults into the air on two feet
rampant)

the sphinx
relaxes
couchant
waiting for time
to happen
feels no anxiety
to make it happen
vaulting ready
to attack

is not rampant

AFTER RODNEY

I

Black Friday

Do you not fear
who sent his ashes on the wind
that ashes blow
more wild
than words?

do you not fear
who blasted out his fertile source
that scattered seed
will like the sower's
grow?

does not the phoenix image
fright thee scholar mind
and walls of Walters
threaten nightmares
to your bed?

do you not father
fear who left his young ones
fatherless
the future of your fathered young
stung with the poison
of their latent rage?

Pray to the gods
to intercept their hands
and know your children
guiltless then
and free

II

From the Wife

I have no tears to weep
the time is wrong for fruitless tears
that will not water
ashes back to blood

when tears might urge some justice voice
I wept in vain then
tears brought silence
while I dreamt
the furious fire
of this end

So now I keep my tears
their salt to season
my resolve
preserve my centre whole

dawn breaks again
my children
come

CONVERSATION

'Earthly love makes for leaving
if you came and left me
I could die…'
                    (Goodison)

So now love
after hours of
burning issues
after late night
mystic notes
sweet on the marimba

here where the night wind
skirts along the waves
lets not love
take these short intoxicating breaths
lets long cool lungfuls seacharged
that refresh and heal

For I shall need your shelter friend-
ship everlasting green
like leaves of mangrove
fed by brackish waters
where the river gives itself
up to the sea

      not love
      so frail
      it dies at day's end
      or at first bloom
      like the yellow poui

And I shall need your ever-
lasting nurture
not that reaping which consumes
without the phoenix power

      So no love
      not love
      now

CARET BAY I

Stone cabbages
fullformed from rock face
burst endless
underneath our feet

stone flakes in layers
near overhanging cliffs
make silkscreens
everywhere

so little sand here
craglets looking out to sea
and this one boulder
(from another time?)

come smell the evening
fires lighting
under irie pots
where cabins hide

stare through the bamboo
fingers long enough
for upright logs
we missed before to show

like this encounter
almost missed
now held and savoured
here.
Give thanks.

CARET BAY II

Looking for a metaphor
to mark our evening
stretched out over
rocks that slope
patterned into a shallow sea

I stumble upon
pure spring water
gently rushing
down grey crags
caught in our cupped hands
pressed to thirsty lips
for inner healing

These metaphors are empty
played over drained
down centuries of bards
'O for a draught…'
'Drink deep or taste not…'

This evening needs no syllables
to watch us walk away
shielded by sombre evening
and the smell of young smoke
rising like incense
from a dreadlocks' hearth

taking with us our memory

and awe

HEAVENS CHERUBIM HIGH HORSED
OR THE MEETING OF THE TWO SEVENS (May 1977)

Poised smiling on your charger
high striding on your stilts
my mokojumbie
god among gods
made flesh and carpenter
teacher and gardener
words man
sounds man
life man

I might have missed you
Mannnn
I might have missed
your vacant mystery look
collecting images
vibrations
I might have missed you
god!

You found me out
measured my acres
chose a site and
bam! implosed upon me
many mouthed concerns
onions azaleas
cows and compost heaps

I find my spirit dancing in my head
I find me whirling to your many strings
and do I see you spinning on your stilts
burning the pure glint of your steady eye
deepening the hollows angel fingers
pressed into your cheeks?

You feel I know
but something surely
smaller than my awe
you had no search
how then could you have found?

I sought a man
a black man with his head
still firmly stitched into his black resolve
no jiving teeny bopper
overgrown with time

I found you mokojumbie.
frightened… with faith I touch your rib
and spin again to scream
'It's real!'

JOURNEY AND FRACTALS

Easy
the DC9 along cloud road
white and smooth today
like boat gliding on blue

clouds like Virgin islets
part to give pass

sitting here
bolt upright seatbelted
I live again the pace of steady climb
up from Bordeaux
out from the underbrush
to steps that led
so long ago
to the not-so-great house of some
not-so-wealthy fellow
planting indigo in Tap Hus

And the climb is repeated
five times over
over paths of identical red
'if you blindfold me and leave me in one
I would certainly think its the other'

Now after Mandahl Bay
us humming Bob Marley
from Dorothy's album
propped proudly
near her bed
and we affirm our shared awakening
at different points on a Washington/New York
late sixties map

and I dont care how many times
you have done this with how many others
for it is only mine
this that you share with me
Bordeaux and Mandahl and Bob

it is in rugged journeys that I know you
not brother nor lover
but morning shadow
double cast in height
double in depth
of all things
feeling

and I give thanks for fences
fallen from round my life
to leave me free
to follow dog-like
in and out mysterious islets
with peculiar names
mysterious rock-shapes with peculiar faces
making pictorial record
of earth's wonders here
these fractals
broken bone and flesh of rock
in rearranged array

and finally the sea
cleansing Coqui
before the scenic ferry
islands Congo and Lovango

and St. John

AT RAW, SUNDAY

and now oh Father
bless this house
whose spirit
calms my soul
this personal Sunday

raindrops
patterning
the silent second
hand gold on brown wood
in stylised crucifix
flush with the altar/wall

seaweed discrete
dried grass
spouting from urns
remembering pagan Greece

But most of all
PEACE…

grant him
oh God
the master of this manor
that inner peace
his mansion
grants this sinner

CONVERSATION (AGAIN?)

Sunset
near rock-
face sea
smoke rising like incense
deep silence of towering trees

In the spaces
between sparse words
I feel us touching
without flesh and sinew

tree rock and everlasting sky
and the great sea

benedictus benedicat

later
we try in vain
for mutual words
to tell us more
than that the clock
the train the bells of evening
hail our parting
fare thee well

yes there should be time

later
much much later
time and time again
the giver gave
give thanks

'Oh soldier soldier
will you marry me

with your musket fife and drum
Oh no sweet maid I cannot marry thee
for I have no clothes to put on'

Oh no sweet man I cannot marry thee
for I have no clothes to put on

It is the closeness
not the clothes
we keep
for clothes bear rituals
bickering and bills
and the slow certain loss of centres
horseheads of childhood
centaurs wait there
round the bend
I hear their bamboo fifes
forcing my feet
to rush me to my hiding

> my mother has no bed
> I have no mother
> under where then
> might I try for shelter?

So let us go
let us go long
feeling the feeling
in the spaces
of our evenings
in this evening of my living
pausing to stare to nod to pinch each other
now and then
touch wood
touch God

from

THE BEST PHILOSOPHERS I KNOW
CAN'T READ OR WRITE

2001

AFTER HEARTEASE NEW ENGLAND

(for Lorna)

It's not no bird
trapped underneath no bridge
it is a soul bird
wheeling towards a springe

Lord teach wings how
in the stark silence of these evenings
in the fine chiselled rock spaces
to fold and nest

'use me oh Lord
use even me...'

for I have heard
so faintly given
the soft/loud cry
for small/large ease

the blue note given
the bird
with swollen throat
receives and gives
the perfect yellow note

THE BEST PHILOSOPHERS I KNOW
CAN'T READ OR WRITE
(for the Lady of Mandahl Peak)

She is large
this migrant mother
and round

like earth
or naan from the tandoori
or saada roti
Indians who could buy
fistfuls of flour
fingerfuls of lard
and little else
made in their new lands
or broad cassava bread
the gentle island Indians
sneaked to hungry blacks
staggering off
murderous ships

She is a maker
hot lunches and hot clothes
cooking and stitching miracles
with equal hand

the hand she writes
unlettered
but the philosophy she speaks
so sound
this mother
pragmatist

to you my son
legitimate

this vast top story
of this useful house
to you my daughter
not legitimate
(yourself now feeder)
I leave the next —
so long as him have floor
you will have ceiling —
rent out the bottom flat
and pay the taxes
render to Uncle Caesar what is his
before him come and seize way what is yours

I wasnt born here
she said softly
weighing her words
resting her elbow on the window sill
and gazing out the window
on the landscape yonder

when I come from
one of these rooms
was house for
me my mother father
and the other five

this hill?

Is lunch I used to bring
help down the basket
salt fish and casi
boil food
and cool mauby
and slap the hand
of fast man building on the site

One day I stop to wipe the sweat
(for disya hill no easy)
and when I look down see the place
so wonderful
and how the sea just sit down calm and clear
the turtle island park up right in there
(you ever up here on a moonlight night?
nowhere no how no moon no pretty so)
a just decide a have to buy a piece
and as a hear me say it in me head
a laugh out loud and look round was to see
if any fast-mouth somebody hearing me
poor poor me one down-island gyal
where me would look
to go and get money?

The story lasted all that night
but it was good that I should know
for I had often wondered how
amid white people
landscaped structures
dogs of high degree
this grand earth mother
house that grew
like Topsy without plan
dogs but pot-hounds
sans pedigree
yard a storehouse
for old decaying cars
and neat new waiting lumber

settled herself
elaborate
half bare
spread out on her verandah
without fear

dared
resting her favours on the rail
to lean or sit there
calmly
taking air

MARINE TURTLE

(for Evelyn O'Callaghan)

In silver half-light
beamed from wave to shore
a flattened hound
bounds from one sandhill
to another sand

frightened
I turn on trembling heel
and flee

The moonlight silvering her coat of husk
the turtle mother
lumbers in the sand
scratching like cat
making his private hole
scratching and stretching out
this clumsy paw then that
until the sand engulfs her in its tub

and now and here
she lays her precious eggs
to bear her light years forward...

Counting off her hope
if one of six
will brave the friendless stretch
will crawl the fearsome sand
and safely back to sea
his birthing done...

covering her new birthed loves
with tender sand
she shuffles back to sea

terrible with hope with fear
tuwhoo the night owl sadly warns

the fisher is hungry for your flesh
the fisher is hungry for your turtle eggs

How could I flee from such a game of hope?
What could I fear from such a sacrifice?
This mother mothering against fearful odds
turns my uncertainties to certainty
in danger yes
but not endangered I

BIRD

Just a dead bird
resting between the shoots
the odd ants crawling in her eyes

was there a shot
some schoolboy with a
catapult perhaps or
springe that caught
but not enough to stop her heart
and let her die there then

she must have
hobbled to my garden
bed shaded by poinsettia green now
waiting to bloom
red and forever young

or was she old
a bird's three score and ten and
chose my garden
to breathe out her last?

whichever
who will tell her mate
her children and her friends
that here she lies
and never will return
clutching her errand
underneath her wing?

so let me leave her there
through morning
noon till evening
and the sun gone down...

One sister flutters near her
checks her pulse(?)
another and another
strangers perhaps
or neighbours
the birdgram now goes
barbling to the clan
sad news sad news…

two concrete blocks
conjoined
make her mausoleum
the earth too wet
might ruffle up her feathers
wet her blue grey wings

so neatly covered now
away from heat and damp
the lady barbledove
(a little portly now I lift her in)
rests on her side

no crows will hanker after her
no ants continue to destroy
her simple eyes
here she will dry and
slowly slowly
underneath her wings
the solid bird flesh yield

NAME

(for Nancy Morejón)

I lost my name
running in the rain
and nobody knows
who I am

sister of India
I hear you
see your unshed tears
like bright round marbles
tense as if those eyes would burst
telling the tale of that one female
wrestling with death
('I will not die until I know my mother's name,
shame shame upon me that I do not know')

and the whisper passing from male to male
her name? her name? her name?
and death taking her
freezing those eyes
wide open
anxious
still

I lost my name
running in the rain
and nobody knows
who I am

sister of Africa
I kiss you with wet eyes
I kneel to greet you
bruising my knees and
spilling easy blood

on unpaved paths
and the innocent blood
of a thousand children
mixes with my bruised blood
staining the paths of
all your dread Sowetos red

limping my protest
I join the march
for justice and right
and the ancient name on the sacred earth
that your fathers have told you was yours
from the beginning...

I lost my name
running in the rain
and nobody knows
who I am

Frieda I feel your eyes
hold useless tears
talking about Elmina.
It is my past
you talk of
slaves packed tight
in space you say should be
your great grandmother's kitchen
and kitchens now you say
will never be the same in Amsterdam
because you felt Elmina...

groans of negroes
turning in narrow rows...
a thousand dreadful holds
a thousand nameless ships

I lost my name
running in the rain
and nobody knows
who I am

Sioux sister
yes I know
I must not tell it
it's YOUR tale
you say
you cannot now reclaim
what to your shame
you lost but
'promise me'
your great grandmother whispers
weeping out her last
eyes glazed and
fastened on your eyes
'you will return our name
to this small patch they call
reserve'

It's not too late
I say not yet
too soon to so despair

name
rain
shame

I lost my name
running in the rain
and nobody knows
who I am
I am
I am

WOMAN IN GOTEBORG
(with a basket on her bicycle)

Is there a tape-
recorder in your basket
lady?
Is there a…
(How can I say that simply
in English the so franca
lingua here?)

Is there a radio
playing in your basket?
Is there a…?

she doesn't answer
she cannot answer

the lady
resting lightly
on the edge

is sobbing loudly
sobbing deeply
sobs with wound-marks
fringed with names

gh ~gh Ana ~gh ~gh ~gh Ana

The universal woman
pass her language
and her face

the corners of her mouth are white
frothing her anger and her tears

Will no one tell me what she sobs?

Is Ana mother?

my mother is dying. Her lungs are painful at each breath.
I will not watch her cells degenerate the tears dry on her face
my mother Ana

Is Ana child?
my child whose father stole her. Now the man-
manoeuvered courts
cry unfit mother! manic mother!
Ana my little Ana

Is Ana wife?

nubile choice of husband/lover seeking change patting
his petty ego (and his paunch)?

Ana how could you Ana

Which universal
woman story
sobs to tear a heart out
from a woman's head
bent to a windy basket
on a bicycle
in a green city
so far North?

NIGHT-FLOWERING CACTUS

so you will come...
perhaps tomorrow...

for I can smell you strangely
tingling my sneezing
through the evening

so I will wake up early
before the sun...

while your white slender
strips still stretch
taut from the yellow centre

while bees still
jostle pausing in their zing
to clutch your dust

Tomorrow
fallen in
phallic rest
you'll hang

only your sepals
still
will stare
and watch another you
burst brilliant
briefly

before the sun

OLD AGE

(for Mervyn Morris)

Our assets
like our limbs
shrink

the house
becomes apartment
becomes room

time shrinks us
to the tomb

A KIND OF DYING

I

My father
as his muscles fell away
might well have chuckled
with that wry humour
we had come to know
'this is the best
that I can manage for you'

no fuss
no call the doctor
foolish
needless needles
drips
and endless waiting
round the saddened sheets

it has to be one day
he used to say

dramatic to the last
here, draw the curtain now
he said
for I must be alone
to play the end

he had known suffering ever-
lasting pain
never so bad to die from
never so good to feel
the luxury of ease

for me
it is enough to know he had
surprise!
one golden morning without pain
one little heaven then
before he closed his eyes

II

I choose cremation
I like the certainty
of such a modern certain means
in such uncertain situations

years after my mother
I would see her
suddenly sit bolt upright
and say
with undisguised surprise
'my gospel they have left me'
forcing the lid from off her coffin
watching the ceiling of the close
clay house they gave her for bone-keeping

somewhere perhaps
I had read of skeletons
men buried prone
found fleshless
and poised foetal

So let my ashes
be to ashes
mingling with the earth
as nicely as my rotting flesh
with other choice
in time would mingle with it

A SCIENTIST SPEAKS OF RELATIONSHIPS:
THE SNAKE IS HIS METAPHOR

the boa
not constricts
does not
choke flesh to death

wraps lightly
gently rings
its prey

breathe in
the boa tightens slightly

out
the breath is shorter

in
the boa tightens slightly...

slowly
the boa
gently hugs

the victim

breathes
to death

ARMAGEDDON NEEDN'T BE A WAR

The revolution will come
soon come   they say
the volcano will burst
mus bus   they say

Who says the revolution is not here?
Who says the volcano didn't burst?

is not a pitched battle revolution
you know
is not a machine gun and nuclear bomb revolution
you know
is a guerilla revolution
is a knife and cutlass revolution

Houseowner look to yourself
now
get down on your knees and pray
now
God is your only refuge now

for the man shall come
wearing the shirt that you give him
and chop off you neck
because you
had the shirt to give him

and the son of the woman you lend
bed to lie on
will shoot you
bastard of too many beds
all the time mumbling under his breath
'is six a wi sleep on one bed where I come from yaaaw'

Minimum wage and the price of
bread milk and neck-and-back
raise same time
factory and hospital
close same time

hotel put up and squatters
remove same time

Blood and destruction shall be so in use that...'

outside
in foreign
each country its own Armageddon

Black South Africa
bawling for Chris Hani
murder and more murder (again?)

Bones and blood of little children
staining the streets of
Bosnia and Serbia

Nobody bothers to speak
about the Middle East
or hungry ghettos
soiling North American cities

black like beans on a
white Sunday tablecloth

And everywhere
in international talk-shops
politicians converse
about aid and equality

MAYA/CHICHEN ITZA

Stone piled on stone
Columbus saw
and seeing said
'Perhaps they hoped to reach their heaven so.'

his little mind
their little minds
Columbus and all bosses after him

all they could see
here on this awesome site
was hopeless stone

how many million Mayas disappeared?
how many architects who drew exacting plans?
how many engineers who looked at them and built
while soldiers drilled
and unsung labour heroes
lifted stone to stone?

how many artists
carved these holy eagles
holy serpents
feathered leaders heads?

While scribes wrote history even now unread
brave men were playing to their death
bare chests were sweating in the corn

young backs bent coughing among formless stone
and women squatting stoic gave quick birth
while hammocks curved with new loves mating

They couldn't write my write
the white man said
nor read my read
as if that's why
they died

Xunantunich
Tikal
Carthage and
Ancient Rome
all these (and more)
were equally
for some great people
home

BRIDGES

An old man with serious eyes
tells me they want to build
bridges to join
pleasure islands in Lake Ontario
to mainland Toronto

'for emergencies' he says

At home I find them waiting
waiting to build
bridges over water
ten feet of new water
sprung in yesterday's plantation

waiting for new bridges
to join villages
near flood-washed Port Antonio
bridges to bring nutri-buns
bridging hunger
O my children

But he
that old man with serious eyes
is urging bridges

for emergencies

ELDORADO

cows grazing
knee deep
in mud flats
along the coast

boats basking in sand
until the flow tide
rides them out to sea

mountains unseen
unless you fly
to villages
whose names you cannot say
Anna, Tumatumari
towards the Pakaraimas near Lethem

Warrau and Arawak
speak still
in tongues
unknown to Anglo black and white...

along the coast
a sudden groan of discontent
the tension snaps
mati go kill mati

failed Eldorado
why?

AFTER TORTOLA

do not weep for me
for
I have seen boulders
trying for the sky
rise from the Baths at Virgin Gorda

refused Mahogany and took Main
Trail through Sage Mountain on Tortola

felt my pores
drink the light brown beer
of Brewer's Bay...

and I have gazed with wonder at Chichen Itza
half climbed Xunantunich
and drunk the sweet sweet water of Gumagaruga

I have seen Hong Kong hills
rise gently from the sea like brush art
murals on a Chinese wall

walked with my daughter
through the Borgia gardens
grateful she was ten

marvelled at steep Swiss rail
rode horse-drawn cabs in Zermatt
under mighty Matterhorn

Over and over I have watched
and never tired to see
islets and rocks
rise silent from the virgin
waters of two different flags

And every time I see
their simple beauty
I give thanks

PORTOBELLO

I stood
where Drake fell
Francis
forever on my mind

I dont remember
how they say he fell
or who (if anyone) felled him
I only know
forever I have felt
this senior pirate
honoured till my time
remembered still
in names of great hotels
and water passages
deserved to fall

somebody must have said
cutting her eye
'dis wan fi ded bad'
here he died
how bad I cannot tell

green hills look towering down
on that fair strand
that looks in turn out to a tranquil sea
from ancient look-outs standing
still (remembering all the El moro
signatures of Spain)

now little children
clamber up the ramp
looking at cannons
touching their rusted mouths

free from all fear
(the smell of powder
fired from these guns
envelops all my air)

no tablet holds his name
only ancestral murmurs
mouthing words
remind me
here he died
aquí se murió
el falleció
these words in syllables
his spirit does not recognize

yet it is fitting that he should die here
(unless he could die everywhere)
here where a tract of land
links the Atlantic and Pacific
here where best re-
presents all island histories
new nomads wandering...

how could Drake know
that galleons would bring here
slaves yearning to fulfill
dreams that were dreamt
before their fathers' futures
dreams to construct
the awesome interlocking
locks lakes
Canal
that would connect
Carib and South sea
(against divine design?)

this jut of land
making the two worlds one

so here I stand
smelling the blood of Drake
smelling gun power
seeing mingled sailors soldiers
spirits pushing metal…
feeling this deep and
satisfying end
conclusion to some things

Drake did die here
and while I smile
small children stare and wonder
whispering underneath their hands
'la loca'

from

LEAVING TRACES

2008

THINKING RE-THINKING BATHS, VIRGIN GORDA

I: (1987)

Peter as rock
(on which I build my church)
was good enough for Christ
in Palestine

here rocks build
Cathedrals
a thousand times the breadth of man
ten times his height

the Father playing blocks
with rocks

sometimes they are ample beds
whose canopies are trees

and sometimes rooms
where lovers hide from envious eyes

sometimes they fall into the bay
make sandy coves

these baths
that give this rest its name

where little children fearless
dive from rock to sea floor
laughing

II: (1988)

Batholith
its rocks
now lit with sun shafts
beaming over myriad
baylets

bathers
each in his own cove
bask in its salt
sand and crystal sea

who knows how sprang
these rocks from out the deep
or when?

who knows how soon
these rocks return
to sea floor why?

centuries of calm
will hear their low complaints
gurgling like sea-shelled water
how little children
scrambling up
chipped bone away
leaving serrated edges

how drunken boaters
entering from the sea
flung beer cans wine casques
stuck there now
these shards of copper colour
faking nature
art by chance

while creatures ever sea-borne
hold their sides and laugh
and unbelieving whisper
underneath serrated hands
lies lies…

III (1998)

Again these awesome rocks
this Batholith
these Baths
that terrify and soothe

again this helpless
facing nature towering here
how small a thing is (wo)man

mark the cool
early morning silence
all human out of sight

lying low perhaps
in boats riding at anchor
or circling the slow bay

lying low
to wonder at the sea carved
face of giant rock on rock

Later the sun comes
bringing Columbuses
with back-packs and blubber
gazing at rocks they dare not climb
(footholds too few and far between
rockface too smooth)

close your eyes
listen and hear
waves breaking gently near the shore
inhaling loud
exhaling soft

until the boom box
cracks the almost silence

Music however sweet
disturbs the meditative mood
beach and the Baths get littered now
selling T-shirts
with music sun and ice

MONTSERRAT
(May 1998)

I: Old Town

curtains still move
where wind blows
cooling windows

yards swept
doors barely shut…

parents will come
home here

anytime now
children banging lunch pans
will prance up these
stone steps
hurry to rooms
throw school bags down
rush out…

No

for the ash is piled
in heaps
where flowers and weeds
fight for supremacy

and neither child
nor parent
will come home

a bar divides
safe from unsafe

the hill slide is smooth
unrumpled
where liquid turned ash
poured down

and unlittered
except for bare bones
here and there

the town is silent
like sleep

while Vesuvius of the Antilles
still smokes
ever so slightly

AT THE HORTOBAGY NEAR DEBRECEN
(for Cecile Carrington)

Sheep
with light brown curly hair
laze here
like sheep
at ease

in pens
with patient pigs
whose manes
lie straight and black...

Unloading from the
horse-drawn buses
us...
from many countries
gawk
at sheep
with brown and curly hair

creole I say
mixed breed
hybrid
high breed
of language
people
sheep now

creole sheep
I say
these pigs are parents
too

scornful
they answer
doesn't she know
species dont mix

creole
I stubbornly repeat
sheep

Science
without imagination
quite ignores
the likes of Minos
Leda with the swan
or Hindu
Ganesh with his elephant head

still science cant defeat
(I think/ wink)
white sheep black pigs
oink oink

in heat

TRENTO
(Fall 2000)

I

no radio yet
so music here
is rain
and rain itself
is foreground
background
base notes and treble
trembling
fortissimo
to cobbled streets
enticing
easy sleep

until
the shattering TV truth
of rivers
giving up their banks
and thousands newly homeless

weather-mongers
sigh and wonder
when and where
the Po will empty out itself

the rain
entices me no longer
now I watch and sleep
and struggle to believe
the last great
finalizing flood
was Noah's

II: *Rain*

This rain…
she said

I spent
I said

September once
in England

Strange
I watched
the river
flood
the flood
like huracán
Trento
October

October
I sighed
all over

you brought
the rain
she said
we never…

November can
and has
I said
but who can prove
the mind's
prediction

till the eye
storms in

III: *Train to Venice*
(for Evan Wilson)

Sticks
like crossed swords
protect the grapes
for mile on mile
beside the Adige

this river
gentle now
the last week's
threatening turbulence
turned history

beyond
rock mountains
making castles, temples, shipyards
cities of the mind
with here and there a real one
(castle)
firmly stowed

It is October now
no snow
or very little on the peaks
sunlight and bright pink foliage
peep from over rock
from time to time

From Rivereto
Venice bound
this dream
some thirty years begun

Catullus' gem
(O Sirmio

paene insula)
yesterday's surprise

Sirmio
where vowels stretch
and curl up at the end
closer to Rome that sound
than Celtic Trent
with its teutonic blend

Today's is Venice
ancient waterways
and hand-shined gondolas
now worth their weight in gold
Piazza San Marco
higglers here
like cities everywhere
the same fake brands
the same importunate hands

the Rialto
remembering Shylock
and his crowd
then the trattoria
almost hidden
in the cool arcade
treat of Venetian fish

and later
in and out the
several other arcades
to Tiepolo's scuola…

at home
Tiepolo's Walcott hound
sits waiting…

IV: *On the corner in Trento*

Perhaps a book
in hand
to say
this wistful woman
standing
is not
soliciting

no sister
seeking favours
just a woman
waiting
on the corner
by the bread shop
(paneficio: I make
efficient bread!)

where a car
her friend
will pass
and take her
anytime now
home

(cant take her
from her door
a city door
on favoured
cobbled streets
where rules say
cars cant come)

She's old
you say

and street women
are young
but who
I ask you

who will guess
a woman's age here
where she's black
(you've seen one
haven't you
further south
in a museum)

men   yes
arms full
of trays
with trinkets
selling

no
pretending that they sell
set up with dignity
black beggars
ageless
after apple-
picking
waiting to go home
to Senegal, Algeria
any Africa

But they are men
so tell me then
how should
a woman look

perhaps a book...

CUT LANGUAGE!
(for Stephen)

Wrapping your tongue
round words
Stephen man-
oevering
'spinsters and
bachelors'

how many learn to spell
but never practise
words
my grandson

you will be
wordsman
claiming this English
language
other people's
anguish

claiming our
patwa

switching easy
when reason calls
'I saw the lightning
leaping through the house
I heard the thunder clap
an Nanny bawl out "Jiizas Krais" '

Children across the wall
offend
and you defend

with 'gwe bwai
no bada wi'

didn't I tell them
everytime
bilingual is the lick?

IT IS THE DYING TIME
(*for Madge Hall*)

It is the dying time
the tall boy writes
counting the dead…

bird on the wing
moves lightly
near the purple sunset deepening

blissful and carefree
bird cannot know
how keen the short boy aims

(another David
with his sling)

This bird
is not Goliath
large and sure

wounded near night
she falls   her gentle head
against a stone

SCHISTOSOMA
(for Emily Krasinski)

Schistosoma
swims through toe spaces
from rivers moving slow
down the archipelago
up through yards of gut

and men with ten toes
innocent of leather
are sitting water ducks

Abijah soon sits nodding
like Taata waiting on his sentence home
or hands still resting lightly on the hoe
dreams off

and even I
parrotting Maasa's verbiage
want to know
bwai how you can sleep so?

He died too soon

I weep
now that I know
the nodding nigger
Schistosoma

had

to nod so

WHILE TV TOWERS BURN
(*Fall 2001*)

I

Is someone out there saying
now they know?

ghosts nodding out there
now they feel

flames frightening
guiltless sisters
brothers blinded
smoke and dust
and shock?

Who's bombing?
where's burning
London? Berlin?
Iraq, Iran or madmen in Grenada?

a morning's nightmare here

The Pentagon, New York's twin
towers of brick and steel

Who's screaming
why the answering tears?

'It's literally chaos now out there' reporting
reporting reporting
from PS which
school teacher
voices calm
across the inter-

com/e tell
little children
how to
where to
hide

Two planes hit
mokojombie tower
twins a hundred stories
high
screech of
women's voices
ambulances
fire-
trucks casualties...

firemen and cops
go answering children
pointing where to
not to
go

smoke smoke
and flames
remembering
Montserrat puffing
dark grey clouds and
Aetna flaming orange
Summer skies

ring the brigade bell
toll for three hundred dead
firemen charging
brave up stairwells
bright to their last

fire this time!

II

The head of the hydra is cut
The heads of the hydra are springing

Tell them   but will they hear?

You come to me with a sling and a stone?
Goliath deriding died

You tell them
Me they wont hear

high passion pass high tech
for driven and driver are one

tell them but they wont hear
tell them but they dont care

So they bomb the stone mountain
Crack open caves

yesterday survivor was a million dollar dare
today survivor is empty handed, spared

throw the dice now and see
whose luck is out
whose luck is in
terror is terror anywhere
Iran, New York

Port Royal's wreck
so many fathoms deep
(where earth shook up
and not a ripple on the sea)

show them
but will they see?

Hospital people
huddle now
caring the dying:

plane blast
stone splatter
or backlash

as we (?) stab
one young white nigger-
loving bastard visiting (from Australia?)

one harmless ageing uncle
Sikh minding his petrol
station without flames etc. etc.

screaming
America
America
they ask
why innocent
we must defend
a turban
or the right to choose a friend?

III

'Lest we become the evil we deplore…'
this from the Holy Pulpit
the Lord Bishop pleads
to folks and terrorists
the Other from the flaming chair of power finger points
'If you are the friend of my enemy you are my enemy;
our targets have no bases but their harbourers have…'

So mothers' hair will tangle with the dust
falling for sons they never bore
so You can find that face or any face
to take your anger and your hate

Bin Laden
friend turned foe
moonwalks his TV
walk of yesteryear

this face we know
this face we can
recurring scan
long evenings in the family room

the little voice
the powerless voice
insists to deafened ears
'an eye for an eye leaves both men blind'

and so
we going to
bomb them
smoke them
root them out

For collateral damage:
old peoples homes
creches and hospitals
we deeply apologize.

IV

New York, New York
our new connection is to absence
this ash that was our desks our e-mails
and our friends...

shards of sharp glass
of concrete and of bone
mingle with ash
confusing...

striving to reconstruct
we construct stretchers
find no wounded for them
body bags   no bodies to fill them

faithful
fearful hands
dreading to dredge
find foot
traumatic hand here
debris and their dust

WAR CHILD
(after Iraq)

For weeks and weeks before the war
while war threats thundered in the air
I worried
focused on that
globe eyed kindergarten boy
laughing and running
carefree with the wind...
that playground in Tikrit

and on his wide-eyed sister
hugging goodbye
and kissing him
then sheltering clutching
mother's flowing skirt

and after mosque on Friday
friends and family
stealing glances at their innocence...
what if the soldiers freed them?
what if tomorrow?

while macho power brokers
Tweedlebush and Tweedleblair
hugging their own
less wide-eyed
thin-lipped children
plotted freedom

And now my little wide-eyed friend
liberated
lost
groaning in pointless pain
wordlessly wonders

why the boy soldier
sitting near his bed
in this strange hospital
(in Kuwait?)
talks about freedom
in such poor Arabic

why is he smiling?

hallucinations
after nurse's ministration
take my once bright friend
laughing and running
(without arms and legs)
far from the friendly soldier

to that windy playground
in Tikrit

MESSIAH

They say the Messiah will come
someday
perhaps today

and if he comes
when he comes
in Gaza

or looking for
Bethlehem
where

they say
the fake precursor
was born

if he too wants
to live
to be thirty-three

which of the men in the mosque
who with his bayonet drawn
which of the frightened faces

is He?

WHILE THE SAP FLOWS

April comes in
with yellow poui
defining Mona

and this one leafless trunk
a young amputee
basket case
lately returned
(from which wind-war?)
shoots
from out naked nodes
its brilliant yellow blooms

the sap still flows

blooms hug the trunk
that shouts out
I too can!

echoing its note
amidst the yellow branches
of those luckier trunks
who shower their myriad petals
blanketing the earth

And what a message
there for us
whose strides
each early morning
take us past this place

Know this
O doubting heart
that while the sap flows
there is nothing
man cannot

VIEW UP THROUGH HER WINDOW

(for Olive Senior)

There is an oak in her garden
with maple behind

green leaves
on purple
figure on blue sky ground

and there is quiet here
except when bird sounds
struggle with aeroplanes
droning to fade away
finally

or bird flutes fuse
with bass of aeroplanes
and the percussive shrrr shrrr
of wind drumming leaves
light with soft fingertips

In the Fall
she will plant anemones
gardening
no longer in the tropics

gardening and paying for advice
here where no grand-
fathers unasked
instruct us
how and what to plant

Gardening
is costly here

and cold

CLOUDS
(for Stephanie)

Like ducks on blue ponds
like swans at sea
like cotton floating
falling anywhere

like candy floss
like myriad brides
in simple white

like choir boys
like cherubim

clouds
like everything

FALL LEAVES

(by bus to Binghamton)

Barely one yellow
Fall leaf left

barren brown stalks
call Winter in

leaves stripped to mesh
to skeleton
and tree feet standing
unshod in dry
leaves dying
flat on their faces

wind curls them on their sides
train their dry eyes
briefly on branches
curved from there
like sea fans

Yesterday those branches
clutched vainly at their stems
whispering with tears 'dont leave, dont go'

nature so fragile here
and urgent
leaves must fall
and branches weep
and seem to break

and then to Spring again
young other leaves

branches must clutch
those new loves
fondly
say again next Fall
with tears 'dont leave'

CONFESSIONS OF A SON

My father lost me
somewhere between
the smell of leather
shoes and the enchantment of untying laces

Waiting to cross swords
with the tyrant
who would cow her
I man watched
hovering over
Mother

(I four feet high)
standing on tiptoe

Half century later
still I do not know
if culture curbed concern
or if he loved less
than he needed love

I store for her
affection without question
for him respect
with unlove
waiting for compassion

WITH THANKS

('...*ya estamos muertos cuando nada nos toca,*
ni una palabra, ni un anhelo, ni una memoria...'
Jorge Luis Borges)

Somewhere between my soul's brief waking and its death
we loved
blending the moon's eye with our wonder
somewhere between my borrowed youth and its thereafter
we touched
and marvelled
fortunados

So when my delta years
their gentle sands run
warm between your fingers
my skin reflecting my soul's glow
will smooth forgetful of time's touch
and all the marrow of November bones
will warm
remembering
how we loved

NEW POEMS

AFTER 'FURIOUS FLOWER' 2004

'I don't believe in Global Warming...'

but the Atlantic warms
to storms
becoming hurricanes
that rush past South
to North America
swiping
the islands
in between
washing them clean
then on to maiming Cuba
blow away Florida
Florida
Florida

past that coast inland
to Galveston
believe me
even to Richmond
et cetera
et cetera...

'I do not see the HIV and AIDS connection...'

but women one in ten
die leaving babies
babies
babies
wards to bankrupt states...

Where leaders are not wise
the people (literally) perish

That wise man Uncle Nketia
come from Ghana tell us how
the music teacher (Euro
teaching Afro children
eight-note scales
'there's nothing else'
had said
and Afro children
knowing poly-rhythms
smiling sang in Euro-rhythm
up and down
the eight-note scale

'the teacher is himself a fool
the teacher is himself a fool!'

'The only thing they can do is behead people'

Busha Bush intones
touching his own head
make sure it still there
what does he mean?

and unsuspecting
from the
Furious Flower floor
some bright black fellow
writing poetry
counter-claims
low, deep, ironic
'they had to go to Bosnia
to find out
bout ethnic cleansing
but terrorism
never new to us

our brothers lynched
school children burned
each day a struggle just to be

if you be Black.'

COUNTRY MUSIC

(for Nikky Finney)

She'd turn the windows up
hiding the music that she loved
'Music they lynched us by'
she heard her father
whispering in her head

she said

and she remembers
diners not for coloureds
she woman under forty
half my age

We sang our country music
naïve and sweet
my people didn't know
or hadn't read

what history said

perhaps they didn't even know
that blues
that music deep down sad and low
was always black

My people sang and
mixed those musics
without fear

truly our parents
hurried fingers in our ears
to shut out dirty words in

mento music labelling
every phrase a sin

'Hag eena mi coco'
the wailing cuckold
(man who get bun)
sang with tears

'I peep through the creases of the keyhole
an a see Mr. Goosy eena Miss Goosy leg'
the merry voyeur
tuned

basic and base
sans ideology
sans politics of race...

Now country music makers
sing here
stare in wonder and delight
black man black woman child
follow their white words
sing along...

downbeat
mutate them
sweet

through loud car windows
mixed with souped-up engines
smashing silence
every beat

music
to lynch who by?

STOKELEY
(after Nikky)

Beside me
At Grantly Adams bound for Cuba
(someone whispers 'Cancer. You know how cureful they are there')

still tall
still straight
Carmichael
eyes proud unshifting still

his sixties flash before my eyes
'Go home and tell your daughters they are beautiful.'
he said it then
no need to say it now
I hear it still…

a thousand Miriams pass before us standing there
all black
all beautiful
all taking transportation to
another desk
another beach hotel
another bed

his swollen feet are slippered
cant have long (I think) not even Cuba can…

Beginning at the feet
the body
falters inch by inch
the spirit
stands that spoke
and still speaks clearly past his end
'Go home and tell your daughters they are beautiful'

AT CIENFUEGOS I
(January 2006)

Sunset an orange line
drawn carefully
and shaded in
against the horizon
after the row of palms

*(soy un hombre sincero
de donde crecen las palmas)*

morning after the night rain
sierras newly washed
rise rise and fall
deep blue against the
light blue pale pink sky

majestic silence near
el Palacio de Valle
guarded by palms
the ever present palms
and the new sun
shimmering
(after the rain)
like jewels on the gentle sea

Cienfuegos
not a hundred fires
but some famous
Asturiano
comandante
from some war
(facts pale before imagination every time)

here nothing says
la guerra passed this way
except perhaps the need for
paint to brighten buildings
stuck in time

and in the heart
here people don't forget…

AT CIENFUEGOS II

Yaso missa Khouri
yaso sah
yaso neva sweet
lakka yaso sah

Who could have guessed
that here in Cienfuegos
after so many years
after so many changes
such special slavery
still...

I watch her touch her nipples
touch her dimple-navel
one two three...
she smiles them to him
everything
Missa Khouri, Karlheim
Carlo (does it matter which?)

her silver ear-
rings pierce the black...
gold threads of hair come
dangling past her face
touching her slender neck

this *tio* doesn't need to hide
his gray hairs
folds of skin
or taut round belly risen
level with his nose
(though he's stretched out
full-length on beach chair
twiddling ecstatic toes)

nor she to hide her youth
her tolerance
her need for things
his age can buy

so many years
after forced crossings
after plantation sun
after the revolution
this voluntary slavery won?

Yaso Missa Khouri
here Sir. Yes

*   *   *

How dare I wonder though
I who should know
'at home
the green remains'
but beachboys
black skins
shine and
white teeth
glisten
muscles tense
striding the beach

parade their hope
stand waiting to
perform
enjuvenating acts on
tias twice their age
ten times their wrinkles

partners pretend...
tell lies to children
asking where
their beach-boy fathers
these days go

later up north
(across the Atlantic too)
tanned *tias* morph to
mothers, sisters
businesswomen, wives

at home
beachboys return as
fathers husbands sons
working the hot-sun land

who colonises whom
in Cienfuegos or Negril
so many centuries later
forced or free
so many centuries
after full free?

PENNY REEL GIRL CHILE

Penny Reel O
Penny reel O
gyal yu gat waa penny fi mi
Penny Reel O…

I promise
if you wait sir
I will pay it all
in one
I'll wash clean cook
till the whole debt is done

An yu no gat i de fi gi mi
Penny Reel O
A beg yu shub yu kushu gi mi
Penny Reel O
An mek mi rub out mi penny
Penny Reel O

Girl this is easy
wipe you eye
I'll take it quick
and make it gentle too
no need to fight
an get mi vex…

Frightened
a birdling crushed
she tries to rush
his hard restraining hand
in vain

closing her eyes…
she would not watch
the pale pork stomach
lowering out and in…

she whispers curses to the gods
and curses too the body
traitor
that will let him in

before he stuffs
his towel in her
screaming throat

before he breaks
her body
and her will

rubbing
his Penny
Reel Ooooo
Out…

AFTER LAMOUR
(for Eddie Baugh)

Long time the warner woman
yellow pencils shooting from her head
spikes from her multi-turban
white or red
wheeled like a dervish
through the village shouting
'Sudden Dead!'

pebbles would flee
fearing her leather
laced-up boots
butterflies resting on the hedge
would rise in yellow unison
and separate speed away

man, woman, child have chance to quake
and wonder whose time next
and start a little silent preparation
just in case

Now every death is sudden
gunshot or motor crash
kitchen knife, machete
or the big (sudden silent) C

*   *   *

I turn death columns everyday
stricken with fear
that I might find a face I know
eyes bright still
shining from the page

or worse that
'In Memoriam'
some friend
I thought had merely gone
last year
or year before to foreign
crying crime or the economy
(or both)

might sit there gazing
schoolgirl smile intact
and almost wave at me
wearing the age she chose

after the internal warner woman
whispered (sudden)
tapping on her arm
'your time now, dear'

or an external
tea-leaf reader
warner palmist
taking
piece of paper from her apron
wrote...

folded the paper
gave her
whispering
sadness in her eyes
'don't open this
till you reach home
my dear'

LETHAL YELLOWING

(for Marjorie Denbow
and so farewell)

that the signal of death
could be so beautiful
so (all limbs) bright
so golden crown
palm spread out
pointing skyward
lethal fair

announcing death
the kingdom of the plant
is passing strange
(plaantin waan ded im shoot)

in man
the body fades
consumes itself
to nothingness and pain
blessing the end
that comes
in its worst hour

the coconut tree
stands lethal in its glory Lord
arms raised adoring up to heaven
so dying
worships thee

WORDS

(after Baugh again?)

Radical
she said
or palliative
the surgeon will decide

and I
with sinking heart
listening
will never know

whether she knew
their different weights

choosing to weigh them equal
for my sake

or did not know
so gave them equal weight

AFTER 'LIMBER LIKE ME'
April 2007

Pam writes about the
cancer necklace
round her father's throat
she must be right
but there's no record in my memory

yes I see pillows
near the corner
see the cylinder
tank of oxygen
level with his head

but most of all
the kindly old man's face
masking his pain

a gentle face
fine white hair
silk and straight

the tired master-fixer
giving up at last
no more re-tyreing now

(never for him the airport wheelchair
not the call to rest
what else is there to fix?)

I never saw him frown
perhaps he did in private
I don't know

A man for everyman
and at his funeral
watching the crowd that came to say
'Respek'
you couldn't guess the colour of the corpse

MY HUSBAND, HIS MISTRESS LIES DYING

Watching you grieve, my love
I die a thousand deaths
and death now has dominion over us
not death but dying
weakening towards the earth...

Always I dreamt of your end or of mine
but not of hers
and surely, not like this
for she was like the trade winds
constant gently sure...

So now I watch your brief uneven sleep
your hurried exit
as the dawn peeps out
to help her mark another grateful day
another vigil
for a hopeful night

whoever wrote that death is penalty
I live each day the torment and the pain
this triangle of pain
hurt flesh hurt mind hurt mind
death dominates
and thwarts the smaller business
of our legal life

The future fades
life is no dome of many-coloured glass
a shattered rearview
mirrors broken pasts

EGO

(or I wish the woman would keep quiet)

The lecture is to seated silence
mostly
This woman though
so sure the audience is
she
asks questions
answers them
speaks to the images on screen
speaks
words across the speaker…

phrases that seek no answer
get her 'tell me!'
statements her 'yes!'
or nod and 'right!'
(Revival style?)

Forward straining on her seat
eyes fixed
challenge to speaker
as to audience
words fiercely pouncing…

Lady
do you hear yourself
your single voice
so public
lady do you care?

Come question time
the speaker silent now

You guessed
she grabs the floor...

From all the egos
like this woman's
Lord
deliver us
and us
and us

NOT IN THE LOO
(AA 331)

That girl across the aisle
is painting over
painted face re-
lining eyes and finger-combing
hair already straight
and yellow streaked

So much have I forgotten
in more years than ten
I have forgot the movement to the loo
the fifteen minutes
till the pilot urges
cabin crew get ready for descent
the necessary gloss
to greet that special greeter
waiting on the ground

Those days we used the loo
she has her mirror clutched by finger-
nails hers and not hers
and sits there preening in her seat
jittery with expectation
frankly oblivious of the likes of me

Believe me madam
I too used to preen
but in the loo

SUGAR SWEET
(Dec. 2007)

try Equal
try Splenda
(poison your body slowly with aspartame)
try Stevia
that's natural
in any case avoid sugar

so say physicians
conservative
or alternative

My hurt is deep
psychic and physical
whole generations altered
for this substance
now 'not fit
for human consumption'

Selah

I CONFUSE
(July 2004)

Behind my back
they massacred
my tressled leaves
my shade
my comfort
day and night

took my protection
took my privacy...

Could my lush
laughing leaves
have guessed
predicted
such a fate
so suddenly?

And I
open to neighbours now
to pointless idlers
and the midday sun
sit tearful thinking...

with what thoughtless ease
some nameless they
disturb my karma
upsidedown my world

don't feel
and so don't even whisper
'Sorry Mrs. Dawg'

PROHIBITED TO TALK ABOUT

(Miami Airport Concourse A)

Prohibited to talk about or carry the following items
Gun, mace etc. etc.

I hope to hold this notice in my head
long after *Ebony Newsweek Prevention*
Gwendolyn Brooks
of Furious Flower etc. etc.

Prohibited to talk about…

It is America after all
land of the free
people not words…

I idle after coffee
tire of hearing
cell-phone conversations
Anglo Franco Español

here where all language
congregates
to finally confuse
the monolingual yous of A

five hours on any train
is simpler now
for laptops stay at home
cant take the stress
the search
the everlasting
airport terror…

tax-free and duty-free shops
shout 'Guess Watches'
showing long-line-see-through
lace brassieres
black lace and nothing more…
so woman where's the watch?

II

Prohibited to talk about

Miami yes
but me
no spirit for such words
such super politics
it is the personal

I miss…

your turns around the city
patient walk along the beach
long slow strides
humouring me
short-stepping at your side
Miami new
Miami even beautiful

But that was long ago
the time is ugly now and dull

don't want to stay no more
want to go to your two-room mansion
watch the news
eat take-out food
Thai spiced or something simpler

gorge on tsunamis tides
fractals and chaos

the city is empty
sits here
silent bare

Prohibited to talk about…

IN THE HOUSE OF MEMORY
(*St. Thomas V.I. April, 2005*)

Saba...
did we not clean up Saba once
once long ago
claiming
environment
cleaning
where others left
their picnic crumbs
juice boxes, paper, rags?

Was the sea then so rough
pitching and tossing
not this same boat
MacLean II
(those days McLean still lived
and rode his motorbike
fearless and helmetted
up slopes he thought he owned
grandson of Drake, godson of Hawkins
seeking other gold
and other goals
textbooks and science labs)?

No change in seascape
undulating mountains
part to islands still
sailboats and small skiffs
glide along the blue
smooth now
and almost ripple free
like clean sheets
Saturday evening's bed

we ride at anchor
gazing out to sea
or swim and snorkel
near the boat
(one seasick lassie cant enjoy this gig)

this older woman
watch her
walking she takes a cane
but in the water puts her goggles on
kicks out into the ten or fifteen feet
and makes it look like home

The birds will come
the tour-guide pilot says
laughing-gulls and terns
and tropic birds
to hang out here till mid-December
(when the tourists come?)

one solo frigate bird
efficient glider
(did he inspire the metal frigate flying further yonder?)
wings in and out our view
so high
so very high

the guide reports one angel fish
big fish and beautiful
and sea-turtles
staying
more here than anywhere...

What do you want to do?
what else?
the rest must stay

another time
another ride
someone is sick
and needs the shore.

CARET BAY
(again?)

And if I say
love lives at Caret Bay
perhaps you will not understand

Or I might simply say that I must go
must go to Caret Bay...

holding my heart
each time the truck
bumps over deep red gorges
down to foam-fringed blue
with gray spume flying

Here first I found sea art
so exquisitely wrought
high above water
patterned fold on horizontal fold
low below water patterned clear
like under glass

thy artist hand Oh God
is mighty here
and everlasting

year after year
I walk this water's edge
and gaze in wonder
at these dappled rocks

grateful my body
still can navigate
round rocks and flat rocks
out to where patterns lie

grateful his body still
walks lithe and strong
(who handles trucks and guides my fearful hand)
his foot still sure

morning rocks
matt surfaces
cool sands
pelicans and peace
at Caret Bay

ESTATE HOME

These woods are yours
'I think I know'

Trees damp with evening rain
tower above the roof
welcoming…

below wild orchids, ferns
bromeliads painted pink on green
protect the flagstones to the rustic door

I have come
('The guest room is ready' the message said)

Inside time talks in elegance
a mother's hand on petit-pointed cushions
tables and chairs
carved carefully
some senior craftsman when?
narratives of family framed in black and white

Raindrops make gentle music
on the receptive roof
over warm tea cups

The ancient guest bed
canopied and carved
birth bed to generations
looks out through modern glass
through trees
out to the sea

Give thanks

ROADS

(Remembering Aimé Césaire)

'Your roads are good'
I heard me tell the great man
asking how a stranger felt
'but yours are yours' he said

inside this chain of islands
roads tell silently
or shout who owns
who does not own

so answering my young guest
veering flustered
from roads surprising good
to roads surprising bad
'I wish your roads were either
always good or always bad'
'these roads are ours' I say
'just like the bamboo beauty
marvel that you see'

This is my land
my country courting death to mangroves
death to breeding fish
to coral and to trees
wasting our permanence for homes to
transient guests who may or may not come

This is my land
Jamaica to the world
high speed
high art
high music and high thought
currents surprising strong

and peerless mountain beauty
leaping my heart anew
tears in glad eyes

the world looks on
with open mouth
these roads are ours

BENEDICTUS

I did not know that I was hungry
till you gave me bread
that I was thirsty
till you gave me wine

and rock and river murmuring benediction
watched incense rising from a censer dread

All who believe
all who ever believed
share this
and

Give thanks

ABOUT THE AUTHOR

Velma Pollard was born in Jamaica in 1937, educated at Excelsior High School in Kingston and at the University College of the West Indies. She received an MA in Education from McGill University and an MA in the teaching of English from Columbia University. She taught in high schools and universities in Jamaica, Trinidad, Guyana and the USA. From 1975 she taught at the University of the West Indies, Mona until her retirement as Senior Lecturer in Language Education and Dean of the Faculty of Education.

She has always written. She won her first prize for a poem at the age of seven, but none of her work went beyond her desk until 1975 when encouraged by her sister Erna Brodber and others, notably Jean D'Costa who sent one of her stories to *Jamaica Journal*, she started sending pieces to journals in the region. She published *Crown Point and Other Poems*, *Shame Trees Don't Grow Here* and *Leaving Traces* with Peepal Tree in 1988, 1992 and 2008 respectively. Her third poetry collection *The Best Philosophers I Know Can't Read or Write* was published by Mango Publishing in 2001. *Considering Woman*, a collection of prose pieces was published by The Women's Press in 1989. It was reprinted as the first part of *Considering Woman 1 & 2* by Peepal Tree Press in 2010. Her novella *Karl* won the Casa de las Americas in 1992. Her monograph, *Dread Talk - the Language of the Rastafari* was published in 1994 by Canoe Press. She has also edited several anthologies of writing for schools.

She is the mother of three children.

An interview with Velma Pollard appears in Daryl C. Dance *New World Adams: Conversations with Contemporary West Indian Writers*.

ALSO BY VELMA POLLARD

Considering Woman 1 & 2
ISBN: 9781845231699; pp. 160; pub. 2010; price: £8.99

In 1989, Velma Pollard's *Considering Woman*, a collection of short stories, fables and memoir, announced an important publishing debut. Now, over twenty years later, a second collection, *Considering Woman 1 & 2*, various and rich in its own right, is brought into dialogue with the republishing of the earlier pieces in a single volume.

Dialogue between its components is, indeed, intrinsic to the organisation of *Considering Woman 2*. Whilst the stories in "Bitter Tales" are very explicitly set in the past, they are often accompanied by present-day women's talk commenting on the story. In "Mrs Uptown" for instance, we learn that a story that begins as one of male abandonment but becomes an account of a woman who finds a good man and happiness, is being told by a now elderly woman to her neighbour at a conference called "Young Women in Crisis". It is clear that the world presented in these pungently written stories of rape, abuse and unsupported pregnancies is not safely in the past. And the balancing sequence of "Better Tales", each of which arrives at some place of epiphany, safety and even contentment, does so in a world where babies are abandoned in pit latrines, where poverty forces families to give away their children, and a young woman has five unsupported children by the age of twenty-five.

If the later stories no longer feel the need to reflect on the process and reception of women's writing (which the earlier collection does very wittily), across all the work is an acutely sensitive consciousness of the consequences of the passage of time. "Gran...", the longest piece in the book, is both a deeply moving account of the consequences of growing old, and a record of a vanishing way of life.

AND STILL IN PRINT

Crown Point
ISBN:9780948833243; pp.: 84; pub. 1988; £7.99

'Reading... Velma Pollard is to encounter an acutely sensitive consciousness grappling, even in apparently lighter moments, with the complexity of experience.' – Evelyn O'Callaghan, *Jamaica Journal*.

Shame Trees Don't Grow Here
ISBN: 9780948833489; pp. 72; pub. 1993; £7.99

Marvin Williams writes in *The Caribbean Writer*: 'Tone and emotion range wider in Velma Pollard's *Shame Trees Don't Grow Here*... *but poincianas bloom* – from disgust, anger, and outrage to celebration, awe, and praise; from questioning and condemnation to understanding and reconciliation. [...] Wildfire becomes hearth in part two where the beauty and life-enhancing qualities of land, sea, and people are celebrated. Throughout, the poet's skillful use of language remains evident in, for example, her subtle, unobtrusive rhymes that lend musicality to her verse; her puns; double entendres; and other word play.'

Leaving Traces
ISBN: 9781845230210; pp. 72; pub. 2008; £8.99

Velma Pollard has developed a significant following among her fellow Jamaicans and in the wider Caribbean world. In this collection she will delight these – and new readers – with her capacity to unite the personal and the political in a seamless whole. Organized into three sections, the collection explores underlying political concerns, such as the impact of global culture and the dangers of unobstructed American power. The poems move beyond these problems, however, ultimately seeking resolution through understanding the flow of nature and urging a celebration of life.

All available at www.peepaltreepress.com